The Power of Poetry
by David Hamilton

Bonker Books

www.bonkerbooks.com

The Power of Poetry

Printed in the United Kingdom

ISBN 978-0-9558184-4-8

By www.Bonkerbooks.com

A catalogue record for this book is available from the British library.

Dedications

For Doris and Ian
My Mother and Father

Contents

Contents (cont.)

Forward

I have written this book of poems for I found it easy to reflect the visions of my mind in verse. They come from the depth of my heart and soul covering many aspects of life itself as I see and understand it. Some touch on the lighter side of life, some reach into the deeper side of life with no holds barred but all are written with meaning and purpose. In many ways the magic of life seems to be fading away in a modern world of confusion and nature the creating power of human life itself appears to be lost in so many minds of today. In a world of so many problems, wars and disharmony are we actually throwing away the gift of life itself in pursuit of a false happiness. Why is our environment falling apart? Why can we not find peace and unity lavished in love of one and all? What is going so terribly wrong with answers apparently unknown? Many of these answers may be found if these poems touch your heart as they touched the heart that wrote them. I can only hope that they do and that the way to a better world can be found.

Uninviting Streets

Drugs in a doorway, death on the streets.
The smashing of glass, the running of feet.
A shroud of darkness, a frightened mind,
a twisted neck looks behind.

An angry face, a vile sound, the drunk-
en thug is making ground.
The flashing blade of a venomous knife.
A would-be assassin threatens your life.

The scent of sweat and alcoholic breath,
A total stranger offers you death.
With a sense to run, take to your
feet, try to find a safer street.

Screeching of brakes, the sound of a gun,
A gangland vendetta, the death of a son.
A broken window, a looted car, the fa-
miliar scene of another social scar.

A distant scream chills the night,
A helpless rape victim puts up a fight.
No one rushes to offer her aid, our mod-
ern life has left us afraid.

This is your life on the streets today,
fraught with danger in every way,
A failing society turns a rusted key,
While the system of our nation creates yet more misery.

A Brilliant Dawn

When you're feeling down
and all alone
the world it seems
No mercy shown.
A bitter disturbance
Inside your soul,
A fragile mind loses control.
Floating in oblivion
Searching for light
Drowning in wilderness,
Losing your sight,
But you're not alone
On hallowed ground,
For your Mother Nature
Is always around.
If you let her in
Your heart to warm,
You will see
A brilliant dawn.

A Poison Arrow

A rich man's playground engulfs the land
Where the poor and hungry no chance will stand
A society failing, simply falling apart
As a poison arrow pierces its heart
The passion for wealth a naive way
Bringing total chaos as we have no say
For the blinkered few who lead the race
With a selfish icon are a total disgrace
The narrow mind that loves itself
As priceless ornaments clutter the shelf
The works of art, the luxury yacht
The gloating desire to flaunt the lot
Your lives are sad with a hollow heart
Turned black inside from a golden start,
While status and power are turning you on
You are the frozen ones doing the wrong
With a balance of wealth so out of touch
Trampled to dust by a greedy clutch
The enigma though is the reason why
For you're only mortal, you're going to die.

The Darkened Street

Do you know how it feels for a man
Walking through a darkened street
As a woman approaches the other way
And crosses over swiftly upon her feet
The feeling inside is a guilty one
Being a suspect when you've done no wrong
The encounter is tense, with relief as you pass
A needless scenario, the heart remains strong.

So why do we have to feel like this?
Who can we trust, who should we slay?
As a lawless society engulfs the land
No longer safe on the streets today
Her fear of him was so misjudged
But her caution he could understand
Yet if any harm had come to her
This honest man would have lent her a hand.

The Beating Drum

With a distant boom
You will hear it come
The never-ending sound
Of a beating war drum

Boom boom boom
The beat goes on
A curse on the world
In a hate so strong

Brother fighting brother
With a misled hand
Blood being smeared
All across the land

Boom, boom, boom
Nobody can win
The killing of a man
Is a terrible sin

Continued overleaf...

In a changing face
Of modern warfare
Dropping their bombs
Without due care

Boom, boom, boom
Destruction and death
Who wants the power
Of another's last breath
In a hail of bullets
On a hunting ground
While the drum plays on
With a sickening sound

Boom, boom, boom
As the innocent die
The death of a son
With a mother's cry

Why why why
Does the beat go on?
Playing out tunes
Of another war song

Theft Of The Soul

The boats set off for the ivory shores
Where eyes of evil peered from within
Devils of humanity boarded those ships
Seeking their prize of the negro skin

Rounding them up with cold callous hands
No heartfelt emotion was ever seen
Stealing their cargo for a distant land
No worse a crime could there ever have been

Chained and shackled whilst dragged aboard
In conditions unfit for a dying rat
Useless resistance could be raised by the slaves
To be crushed by the swing of a bat

Reaching their fate on the banks of America
The soul takers swapped life for dollars
Casting their victims in tight heavy chains
With iron rings as their only collars

Continued overleaf...

In cruel humility they marched the bedraggled
Frightened and scared, wearing eyes of fear
Like hunted animals, trapped and afraid
Where all self-dignity has to disappear

These traders sailed under the British flag
Shipping evil to a far away nation
The flag was bloodied with ultimate shame
With barbaric deeds to a human relation

When passing judgement on the rest of the world
That evil returns in total recall
If nations were built on immoral actions
Then they have no right to judge at all

Lifting the Blindness

a race was placed upon this earth
With open eyes in a gift of sight
Yet so many live with enclosed blindness
Never seeing the power of the light

Only looking at what is around them
Not forming visions of the mind
Never seeking what is purposely hidden
So a truth of life they never find

Who are we, why are we here?
Many may ask in deepest wonder
What created the great human race?
A question blows the mind in thunder

What we cannot see we do not know
But is what cannot be seen really there
Where truth is a quest for all to find
Too many are struck with a vacant stare

Some say this, some say that
So much confusion pickles the brain
The light is found from the inner self
But misjudged words drive you insane

Continued overleaf...

We can only know what we really know
Others' opinion is their source of belief
To find the light is to know the truth
If it is found you will see the grief

A heart will feel the others' suffering
So share in their enduring pain
Eyes will see the eternal torment
Those images will always remain

The light is life not desire of man
Where equality is shattered by wealth
A never-ending quest of gratification
Crushing the soul and the inner self

A misled mind seeks only glamour
As blindness clouds true vision
Only seeing what is shown to be seen
Is that really your own decision?

Souls are destroyed in a race for power
Blinded within a luxury existence
Brothers and sisters of one and all
Are forced to survive in painful persistence

Blindness is the darkness of the world
Where the devil can defeat the good
But the light is there to offer strength
To ignite us all, it truly should

What is the power surrounding this earth
For all at some time can feel it
Only choose to ignore what they cannot believe
The cloak of wisdom will not fit

If a hope is there of something more
Blindness overshadows the light
Sheep will follow the way that they see
But have they received the insight?

Answers lie within the inner self
Not from the mouths of modern power
For they are driven by wealth and greed
So the earth approaches its final hour

Answer the questions to the puzzle of life
Then the blindness will finally lift
Allow the light to touch the soul
So you can feel that special gift

Feeling Her Light

Oh mother nature
You shine your light
You've nurtured me
Through every fight
You've made a boy
A moral man
Now I will do
All that I can
A purpose of life
You have shown
But deep inside
I've always known
The gift you gave
Is now mine to give
You need to care
In order to live
If all the world
Could feel your light
The human race
Could win the fight

The Phoenix Is Rising

The phoenix is rising
He's flying so high
Gracefully gliding
Above you and I

Shaking the shackles
From a life that's so cruel
Way up high in the distance
What a wonderful view

His spirit is rising
He's taken control
The feeling inside him
Burns from his soul

Seeing the world
Now clearly defined
As its splendour and beauty
Shines through his mind

Continued overleaf...

The phoenix is rising
Way into the sky
Its freedom he's feeling
As he's learning to fly

Flapping his wings
Floating so free
Someone is with him
That someone is me

The phoenix is rising
In the shadow of the sun
He's shown me the light
Now his work is done

Nature's Embrace

On a tropical island of magic
That was cast into a crystal sea
Gentle waves licking pure white sand
A shadow lays beneath a shading tree

A tranquil setting, a lonely beach
As a native sleeps on his sandy bed
His tatty straw hat rests on his face
At peace with himself and trouble ahead

A sheltered position obscuring the sun
Provides the haven of relief
In a life where sunshine warms the heart
A soul burns with true belief

He awakens with a stretching yawn
The smile had never left his face
An aura radiating from a simple man
Born from the spirit of nature's embrace

Optimism

The optimist is alive from within
True belief reigns in his heart
A positive mind is lust for life
That he has felt from the start

The optimist clears away a bleak day
Seeing the gift that he was given
Within his moral living soul
The spirit has truly risen

An optimist feels the power of nature
Beating vibrantly through his veins
Her bright and guiding eternal light
For him forever remains

Closing Down

Technological advancements
The face of a modern world
Satellites breaching the heavens
Invading the space they patrol

Radioactive waves colliding
Crashing through the atmosphere
Normal tasks performed by man
Transformed by remote control

Engulfed by computerised systems
Invading the void of the inner mind
Dreams turn to living nightmares
As they slowly possess the natural soul

No longer having to think for yourself
Beyond the safety net of machines
So relied upon by an idle brain
Now create the living scene

A hypnotic show in any front room
The sanctity of a lounging armchair
Remote controllers littered around
Minds dissolved by a flickering screen

Meaning of life just passing by
Obscured by a menacing cloud
The point of an existence fades away
No longer seeing all the shades of green

The Dreamer

If people say you're a dreamer
Remember that they dream too
Once Neil Armstrong was a dreamer
Until unbelievable dreams came true

Without your dreams you have no drive
So the world would be cold and dark
Dreams relay your inner thoughts
That gives a life its spark

The sleeping mind is never closed
Just free of interference from you
Confusing its natural living path
With the pointless things we do

Dreams bring visions from the soul
To the very heart of the brain
True feelings in vivid colour
Recurring over and over again

Within a dream a message lies
As it is created within the mind
Relive your dreams upon recall
Where many answers you will find

Finding The Meaning Of Life

If you never find
The meaning of life
You will never know
Why you are here

For it lies so deep
Within your soul
Being way beyond
Any normal sphere

An internal connection
You find yourself
A living harmony
With emotional tear

If a moral soul
Rules your heart
The meaning of life
May then become clear

The Fireball

A bright flash of light
Catches a roving eye
An awesome spectacular sight
Burns the darkened sky

A firey alien rock
Casts a trail of flame
Not from our own stock
One you may never see again

It briefly lights the ground
Through a speeding earthward flight
With inaudible yet distinctive sound
As it hurtles through the night

You feel that you could touch it
As your eyes are open wide
True universal magic
That touches you inside

For when you see a meteorite
No ordinary shooting star
The image lasts forever
No matter where you are

Nuclear Dream

Wearing grim faces, the deed had been done
The button's been pushed, so you better run
Missiles are cruising, there's been a mistake
Can anyone stop them, oh no it's too late
So now they are heading, to some foreign land
With a sting in the tail, evil of man's own hand
Check the radar, they've sent some back
One stupid error brings a nuclear attack

Scramble the jets, head for the sky
If they miss the targets, millions will die
They came so fast seeking their prey
But the fighter pilots could not save the day
Run for shelter, get under the ground
Get ready for impact, the earth will pound
A frazzling whoosh, a huge mushroom cloud
A wave of radiation so frighteningly loud

Continued overleaf...

A nuclear wind advances to kill
Ready to incinerate anything at will
Panic rising, as people are screaming or crying
The innocent ones, wounded, dead or dying
The searing heat, the sizzling skin
Nuclear fallout is the ultimate sin
An acrid air we cannot breathe
What has happened we cannot believe

The president awoke from his dream to pray
Ordering complete disarmament that very day
A world drew in a huge sigh of relief
As life could continue with new-found belief
An image projected from a heavenly call
For the dream was cast to save us all
But all was shattered in the final scene
For I awoke, to find it was my own dream.

Release Your Mind

What lights your heart, in the game of life
For what reason are you here
What actually drives your inner mind
Along the course of life you steer

Who is at the helm, is it really your choice
When you cannot do what you want to do
For we are caged I think youll find
Within society's crowded living zoo

Invisible bars of iron steal away your soul
As the keepers tell you how to think
So often losing sanity of the mind
Where you teeter on the very brink

Who are you then my friend?
Is it really you in there?
For when asked what free thought is
You gaze back with a vacant stare

Mind control has been fully achieved
Becoming entrapped within society
Shake the shackles and cast the chains
Then just let your mind run free.

The Diminishing Ozone

Oh why oh why must it be
Man cannot wake up to really see
A diminishing ozone we cannot mend
As it starts to break up and reach its end

We are rushing on with industry
Tearing down all that we see
Modern man has done it since birth
Forsaking the effects on a fragile earth

We are changing her face every day
Playing with nature in every way
The signs are there, we should know
How many more signs must she show?

The effect it will have is unknown to man
We should be doing all that we can
The real damage is too soon to count
But sooner or later the truth will come out

So when do we wake up seeing common sense?
Instead of just sitting on the idle fence
Action is needed in the here and now
Where is that someone to show us how?

The ozone's enigma is a great unknown
Destructive seeds have already been sown
To alter something we know little about
We have to stand and all of us shout

To a diminishing ozone we have to awake
Or be helpless and sad as we start to bake
The signs are there if it's not too late
Or shall we just sit back and await our fate?

Hear The Warning

A peacefully free and harmonious world
Is needed by the whole human race
United as one across the globe
Of racial discrimination no living trace

We are all for all and all as one
The children of one gracious mother
Of the same flesh and flowing red blood
So extend an open hand as a brother

Look around at a fragile planet
All the needless sufferings we cause
We need common ground, a united front
To put an end to these senseless wars

Is the world on the eve of destruction
As politicians determine a coming fate
Too wrapped up in paranoia and power
Poisoning a world with misled hate

If the government saw a true full picture
Then how could they live with themselves?
As we ravage every inch of the earth
Whilst it sounds its warning bells.

Senses Of The World

My senses are alive
I feel my world, I use all five
As I ask the questions
For all of mankind
Using my senses
The answers I'll find

The world I smell
Is an overly polluted, cancer-causing hell
When the air that I breathe
Should be clean and pure
Yet it threatens my life
Without a known cure

The world I hear
Speaks to me, so full of fear
For the race it created
Has lost all control
Why tamper with nature
So rip through her soul

Continued overleaf...

The world that I taste
Is bittersweet and alcohol based
Drowning the sorrows
Until you get hooked
Is never the answer
With a mind overlooked

The world that I touch
I feel her heart, it hurts so much
As her helpless children
Can only sigh
For they are trampled in life
By a political lie

The world that I see
Is being torn apart by all humanity
The misguided few
Who lead the way
Have missed the point
So all must pay

Who Are We Tomorrow?

One man lives, one man dies
One man hears a pack of lies
Who should you trust, who would you slay?
As greedy fingers throw morals away

Whose world is it? What can you own?
Nothing at all for it's only a loan
Because mortal man will only die
Relinquishing wealth to reside in the sky

Open your eyes, behold your earth
Was greed the reason for your birth?
The dividing axe they like to swing
Severs souls that used to sing

Lust for wealth overshadows the mind
In financial entrapment forever will bind
Too many then lose the freedom of life
A bitter pill that can cut like a knife

A tortured brain, a shattered soul
Through an aching heart we lose control
Man's own blindness a social disease
Conformed since birth, told what he sees

Continued overleaf...

Adapts to a system, believes all the lies
Stops asking questions then finally dies
A world around him beyond his shell
Now so obscured from his private hell

His idle mind is closing down
A television's illusion his personal clown
Who do we become, this great human race
Just mindless morons with a bewildered face

With shuttered minds closed at birth
Now seeing all things purely for worth
With designer blinkers the west remains
Seeking only riches or ill-gotten gains

We lose our morals, they've upped and gone
For we cannot see we do such wrong
Because in western life the passion of man
Is to own it all if he possibly can

A very sad result of an intelligent brain
Inflicting upon the world only heartache and pain
By polluting this or destroying that
To satisfy the mind of a spoiled brat

Whose connection to nature is severed and torn
Neglecting the mother from whom he was born
Yet nature around him holds the key
But her crying signs he still fails to see

For his misled head was never told
So can only watch the devastation unfold
A ravaged world has started crying
As the tortured earth is slowly dying

All the signs are there to see
Take a look, just break free
Open your mind, open your heart
Think of your world, for that's a start

Mankind came and seized the power
Does the world now approach its final hour
Could the ultimate fate be a living hell
Where it is too late to sound a repenting bell

The meaning of life is continuation
Not crushing the hopes of the next generation
Think of your children, imagine the sorrow
For they may not see a new tomorrow

My Heaven, My Earth

My Heaven, my earth
My world of nature, who paved my birth
To you I bow
And for no other will
You light the way
I follow you still

My world of nature
You are my God and soul creator
The spirit I feel
Is guidance from you
No laws need I
For my heart is true

My sun, my moon
An entire universe, that is all in tune
Care for thy neighbour
Then all will be done
For in nature's world
We are all as one

My endless guiding light
I have seen the hardship of the people's plight
End the needless suffering
Search inside your soul
Share with your brothers
Then your life will be whole

Nature's World

In nature's world the sun will rise
Casting light upon another day
To shine so brightly across the land
With a warming golden ray

In nature's world the moon will glow
As a spotlight in the night
An enchanting beam reflecting stars
A magnificent wondrous sight

In nature's world the earth will turn
Until the day is done
Sliding between night and day
With the return of a life-giving sun

In nature's world there is a magical air
As creatures breathe and grow
The very secrets of nature's enigma
Mankind will never know

Continued overleaf...

In nature's world the scales are balanced
As harmony is created
So all her creatures great or small
Are somehow all related

In nature's world mankind evolved
To walk the precious pasture
As the only creature with the power
To upset the balance of nature

In nature's world man holds the key
For a mind he was gifted at birth
So in our hands we hold the fate
Of our sacred planet earth

The Living Earth

Sunshine returns to the valley once more
As April showers have succumbed
An earth alive, plants reaching for light
To grow serenely beneath a golden sun

While lambs abound in emerald fields
Leaves shimmering in living green
The land awakens from hibernation
Colours will form a natural screen

Life that's reaching out to Heaven
With probing shoots and twig like fingers
To soon be opened in a floral display
Natural aroma that's pure and lingers

An enchanting cycle of life resumes
Until the masterpiece is complete
Whilst the beauty of her pleasant lands
Are laid before our feet

Darkness gives way to morning light
As a life-giving sun will glow
The finely-tuned balance of nature
Ensures a natural world will flow

For all in all we are all as one
A life force in a silken web of wonder
Entwined within a magical life
With a warming sun we are born under

War Game

Distorted illusions of a chessboard
A reflective shadow in the sky
Represents a modern war game
Where the players really die

As an evil cloak of hatred
Enshrouds a wonderful world
As venom spits across the globe
For now the snake has uncurled

As mankind seeks to destroy fellow man
For their beliefs do not agree
Whilst narrow minds are starting wars
Our one world can never be free

Shoot to kill from a long distance
Seeing not the death in their eye
For you cannot face the reality
Of watching your victims die

For when they are your fellow man
Another brother of your kind
If you desire to see their life elapse
You must leave your soul behind

It isn't war, just a show of power
Whilst holding on to a nuclear ace
Littering the sky with war machines
Designed to obliterate another race

Now these are the new modern rules
Do you still have desire to play
Or does the sheer horror
Move you towards a brighter day

From behind a barricade of paranoia
Nuclear supremacy was born
So the great American nation
From heartfelt reality was torn

To cast a shadow of evil
With claws that grip the heart
Weapons of mass destruction
Can only tear a soul apart

The sanity of man falls into question
Meaning of life he cannot find
As only money, lust and power
Excite his hollow little mind

When other nations disagree
Watching a ruthless masquerade
They are battered into total silence
Before continuing with the parade

The game is only halfway through
Whilst we analyse the board
It's plainly clear to see who's winning
With all the points America has scored

Continued overleaf...

So is that it? Game over then
The analysts ponder once more
I do not think so, one exclaims
They may still force a draw

If America's enemies decide to unite
After continued assaults on their shores
In a final act of desperation
They could yet even the scores

But such a move would decide the game
For America will never back down
A jittery finger then pushes a button
In nuclear fallout a world will drown

So if everyone ultimately loses
Then why the hell do we play
No empire has lasted forever
It's as clear as the light of day

At last my friend you see the point
This is such a ridiculous game
Mortal minds of a western world
Have well and truly gone insane

The Sun Rising

Standing on the water's edge
He found himself once more
Whilst the ocean gently laps
The glistening sandy shore

A darkened shroud fades away
Surrendering to morning light
A mystical reddened fiery glow
Scorches the remnants of the night

The earth awakens in yellow flair
Draped in a golden fleece
A portrait hangs upon the air
As nature's visual masterpiece

Daylight gracefully breaking
In the apparition of her crown
The sun heralds another dawn
For she never wears a frown

Slowly rising to stand so bold
With a heart that burns so bright
To once again engulf the land
In precious life-giving light

Crushing The People

Living in a world of wonder
Covered in a golden shroud
A sun we are living under
Obscured only by cloud

But the cloud can be a vision
That's darkening the mind
An inner manifestation
Where light is not defined

For the light is the fire
That ignites the spark of life
To extinguish it in pure desire
The bitterness can be rife

A troubled soul will lose the glow
As the mind is torn apart
Within its torture visions grow
Then soon the pain will start

Continued overleaf...

Vivid pictures within the dreams
Tearing away at the soul
For life is crazy so it seems
When losing the inner control

Slowly drowning, losing faith
Collapsing from deep within
Darkness falls like a devil's wraith
Dragging them into a world of sin

The result of crushing the people
Who only yearn to be free
They can see the top of the world
But for them it will never be

Misled Visions

By the hands of politicians
A future is being designed
Puppets pull the strings of life
As their minds are realigned

Born in wealth and glamour
Education plants the seed
Twisted from a natural way
Sees a life of greed

Shrouded in corruption
Manifested in political lies
Caught in sexual scandal
The power always buys

Through a misled vision
Stupid rules are made
Without conception of real life
In blindness they still wade

Without the understanding
Of people's hearts and souls
Dressed in fancy suits
They stand upon the polls

Very little choice is offered
In whom will stand elect
When no one in the running
Is whom you would select

Society is a shambles
So out of their control
Too many problems still arise
To dig a deeper hole

As little sheep follow along
The trail that they are led
Caught within a restrictive net
Accepting all that's said

The blind will lead the blind
Until the day is done
Far too many politicians
Fail to see the sun

They are seeing only power
Seeking out the fame
Within the only way they know
The problems still remain

Continued overleaf...

Something needs to change
To find a better way of life
Boldness needs to seize the reins
Then cut them with a knife

The politician is one thing
A great leader is so rare
One that stands to do what's right
Without any living care

Until the day a leader rises
With a passion from within
A social furnace rages fire
Puppet strings wear so thin

So think about the people
Consider all their needs
Not the circle of wealth
It's the poorer heart that bleeds

Riches Count For Nothing

What has a greater value
Than the gift of life itself
A healthy living body
Outweighs the sin of wealth

Human life was given
Totally free of charge
Requiring only nature's power
Without the entourage

So why do we seek the glamour
Whilst yearning all the fame
For deep inside the heart
We are all the same

One will rise above another
In their blinded misconception
That sets the ego running
Within a personal deception

Continued overleaf...

For no single man is better
Within these mortal eyes
Where every man is equal
But many words are lies

Was money made in heaven
Or crafted by the earth?
Can a man be truly judged
Just solely by his worth?

Merit lies within the soul
The only priceless possession
If pureness reigns within a heart
It will lose unnatural obsession

Greed is like a noose
Placed around the neck
An evil little poison
Along a lonely trek

Glamour is a fashion
A narrow mind will seek
So blinded by the ego
To rise above the meek

Riches form of gluttony
Within a hollow mind
Creation of a spoiled brat
Is all they ever find

But now those days are over
Because nature's fighting back
Your wealth is just a drug
So throw it on the stack

You can never buy a life
It remains beyond your power
For everyone is equal
Within the final hour

When the wrath of mother nature
Falls upon the sacred earth
She will never be forgiving
No matter what you're worth

But if a God in Heaven
Brings forth a judgement day
Those riches count for nothing
Not even if you pray

The Narrow Gate

Within the distance of forgotten time
A magical mystical world transpired
Crafted through the perfection of nature
Creating the earth as she desired

Has she reached a final destiny
Bringing forth the rise of mankind
Placed upon her precious world
With crucial answers yet to find

There would have to be a purpose
For creating a higher being
A reason for rearing a greater breed
That so very few are seeing

Not many seek the narrow gate
Passing through the one so wide
Caught in a technological playground
The meaning of life has died

Visions obscured by recreation
Of too many misled idle hands
Destruction of an ailing world
Pollutions washed upon the sands

Is this a destiny already foretold?
Was man designed to kill the earth?
Has the end of an age been reached?
Was it destined by his very birth?

What is the point of human evolvement?
Seeing only a life that is sown
To instigate the self-destruction
Or seek for answers still unknown

The end of an age is a prophecy
A destruction already foreseen
Warnings of wisdom duely ignored
Desire has shattered a living screen

Nostradamus foresaw the end of the world
As a human race became enticed
But there have been far greater warnings
Through the power of Jesus Christ

Nations built on Christian values
Have thrown them all away
Reaping chaos across the earth
Now awaiting their judgement day

Continued overleaf...

Will it be by God or mother nature
As an environment starts to collapse
With man too blind to right his wrongs
A living cycle can only elapse

Will the horses ride to wreak their havoc
Bringing plagues with the edge of a sword
Will all the suffering come to be
As we approach the day of the Lord

Words of wisdom in the power of Jesus
Foretold of the coming fate
If faith is held within his words
Then seek for the narrow gate

The enlightened way remains so dark
For the truth is seldom known
Yet the gate is waiting to be found
Where the way cannot be shown

Mind Connection

The subconscious reaches into the soul
As communication with the inner being
A depth of mind we hardly know
Is the power so few are seeing

To search within is to find the truth
In the depths of the human mind
By only living in the conscious state
Truths remain so hard to find

A mortal existence becomes a puzzle
An enigma that is there to be solved
Power of mind is a gifted tool
One that has slowly evolved

Man reached out for a higher intelligence
But desire became his temptation
Growing inside to overwhelm him
Setting a course for his own creation

Continued overleaf...

Technology appeared to alter concepts
As natural life was redesigned
Minds were led on their altered course
The meaning of life was redesigned

When what is natural becomes no more
In a plague of scientific invention
A mind no longer seeks within
Which is defying nature's intention

Did nature create the ultimate race
To become overruled by the machine
With minds corrupted by television
Instead of seeing her living screen

The Funeral Pyre

The magic of nature is all around
In a world of mystical light
Crafted within a perfect balance
Born through a natural insight

A sun will shine to offer life
Embracing the precious earth
Wonders of nature never ceased
From the moment of its birth

Through a course of evolution
Life would slowly form
Raising up the race of man
An ultimate breed was born

Does nature fulfil a final destiny
By creating the human brain
With a living force of power
Where none are made the same

So there has to be a purpose
For achieving a highest grade
There has to be a reason
Why an intelligent mind was made

Continued overleaf...

Could life reach a higher level
That is yet to be discovered
Is there more to a great enigma
If the mysteries are uncovered

Many signs are lost in recreation
To satisfy self desire
Naturality altered along the way
Whilst building a funeral pyre

By seeking deep inside the mind
Free from a life that is shown
A spark of light resides within
That many have always known

The meaning of life remains unfound
For it lies within nature's fashion
What is unnatural was never meant
To fuel the raging fires of passion

What is the truth of a greater being?
Who is under nature's rule
A gifted mind has far more worth
Than becoming a destructive fool

Fantasy Of The Mind

Falling into the world of fantasy
Gently drifting on a breeze
Floating away within the mind
While feeling well at ease

Inner visions relaying illusions
That form a living scene
Dancing through the inner thoughts
Showing on a private screen

Inside the theatre of the mind
Transforms to another dimension
Travelling through a whole new world
Of naturally born intention

Searching inside the inner realms
Discovers a hidden power
Slowly the great enigma unfolds
Within the darker tower

Many eyes are busy looking out
Blind to the light within
Ears are hearing what is turning
Reverberating upon the chin

Continued overleaf...

In the realms of fantasy reality lies
When a mind looks ever deeper
In the generation of its inner self
So awakening the dormant sleeper

Reaching through a subconscious abyss
A puzzle of life is found
Inner powers entwine with wisdom
That is created on natural ground

Crossing the bridge to the inner self
Delving ever deeper inside
Reaching out for a higher level
With nothing more to hide

A brain harbours the highest sense
As the ultimate power of all
Connection through a conscious thought
Whilst creating a stronger wall

Seeing only things that are shown
When never seeking never finds
Without creating a deep inner vision
Then in fantasy forever binds

An Eternal Battle

An eternal battle of good over evil
Where the serpents will arise
Definition in the one or the other
Is lost within the corrupted lies

When what is right is not always good
Where many evils are disguised
Visions alter in a darkening haze
A true image may not be realised

Riding a frequency of hypnotic illusion
Many channels are never tuned
Suppressed within the spectrum of choice
The inner mind forever cocooned

Fulfilment of ever-rising desire
Is losing the moral ground
Misconception of ideal representation
Lets loose the devil's hound

Restraining ropes are easily slackened
Thus allowing the shield to slip
A silent menace seeping under
As blindness causes the fatal rip

Continued overleaf...

So the good gives way in yield
Whilst the balance slowly sways
The curse of immorally crafted action
Manifesting in so many ways

An eternal battle within the soul
Will determine the depth of good
Within the power may be strong
But temptation rots the wood

Evils stalk within a disguise
Coming through an opened door
Poisons overshadow a natural rhythm
For they cannot be seen any more

The light of goodness burns in the soul
It was born along with the heart
The battle is fought within the self
It was from the very start

Tear Down The Playground

A world just keeps on turning
Drifting through night and day
Moonlight illuminates the darkness
Sunshine spreads a golden ray

Sliding between four seasons
During a climatic range
The perfect balance of nature
Is already starting to change

Powers of the earth have shifted
Throughout the creations of man
Who reaches out in idle action
For everything he possibly can

A world shattered by man's desire
Within temptation uncontained
Losing sight of moral restraint
A world cannot be sustained

The magical gift of creation
Is a planet supporting us all
By turning it into a devil's playground
The human race will fall

Continued overleaf...

In what was made all was given
Yet man desires much more
Transforming life in recreation
Now inflicts a fatal flaw

Science hides behind its claims
Of destructive cycles in the past
Yet none before were caused by man
This time around may be the last

A world just keeps on turning
Nature suffers the enduring pain
But she is a power upon the earth
From retribution will not refrain

Science believes it is so clever
But has become a devil in disguise
Misled minds with meddling fingers
Have plotted their own demise

A truer picture lights the screen
Nature's world is turning black
Man cannot unbalance the earth
A higher power is fighting back

To go to war with mother nature
Is a battle that cannot be won
She is the force that can take away
Everything under a life giving sun

Science cannot recreate a world
Money will not see life returned
So what was given has to be
Or meddling fingers will be burned

For a world to keep on turning
Then humanity needs to change
A course of scientific progression
Has altered the natural range

To kiss goodbye to reckless desire
By retuning to a natural sound
Is the only hope of saving a world
Whilst tearing down the devil's playground

One Wish

When you wish, what do you wish for?
Is it for the world, or is it for you?
Would you lift yourself onto a higher level
Or share the fortune in what you do?

If you could have anything at all
What would drive your heart's desire?
Would you change the suffering all around
Or fulfill yourself in the devil's fire?

How would you receive that single chance?
Could you see beyond what the mind has become?
Would you reach out with compassionate choice
Or crown yourself as the number one son?

It all depends upon the inner soul
Through a caring or a selfish eye
One will look with love of the world
The other will believe he can truly fly

Would you wish to become far richer?
Or that the curse of poverty would fall?
Would you wish for a loved one to recover
Or that there was no more illness at all?

The answer as always should be in the heart
If the light of life is shining through
When what is done is done for others
The beat of the heart is really true

Altered State

Within the power of nature
All the answers lay
What is natural really counts
As the future goes astray

Does nature have a purpose
Within the life she gifts
Or is it just a cycle
Upon which she slowly drifts

Is there a higher meaning
In the magic of mankind
Has she set a hidden puzzle
For all of us to find

Ignoring all the evidence
Science carves another road
Altering concepts of the mind
That starts to overload

As technological ability rises
A natural way will close
By neglecting mother nature
The human race of man rose

Continued overleaf...

Reaching into outer space
Still searching for the clues
Reckless dumb-assed cretins
On a mission they will lose

All the answers surround the earth
Not millions of miles away
Man should never leave his planet
Not even for a day

Science is still struggling
To crush a spiritual power
An inconvenient little problem
One it's trying to devour

But as the falsehood rises
The blind will lead the blind
Confusion of a desiring world
That is being redesigned

Only now it is collapsing
As man becomes machine
For interfering fingers
Have killed a natural scene

The question is can it be
That man can rule the earth
Was the causing of calamity
The reason for his birth

Dismissing parts of history
With a magical power described
Beyond the understanding
So in ignorance still reside

Many minds will feel the connection
That surges from within
Looked upon as spiritual dreamers
To believe becomes a sin

Yet when the soul is open
So really feels the light
It knows beyond all doubt
That it was always right

The rest fall by the wayside
Waiting for the proof
Hearing so much bullshit
They will never know the truth

Do You Believe?

If there really is a God in Heaven
So many of us ask today
Then why is there so much suffering on earth?
Why does he let us go astray?

As we look around our modern world
We really have to wonder
For hell it seems has moved upstairs
With a curse it puts us under

Why would God just let this happen
You search inside your soul
For life can be cruel as now we know
As humanity loses control

Perhaps he strikes us with retribution
For desertion of our faith
Instead of the shining light he brings
He sends the devil's wraith

As the darkest hour befalls mankind
It is now we need our God
Our passage grows so bleak and dark
Along the pathway we have trod

Reflections on personal tragedy or pain
Can we blame a spiritual father
For fate does pry into our natural life
Where many need looking after

If we opened our arms once more to Heaven
Then search for our guiding light
We may find we are given one more chance
To put our errors right

In a God we would like to believe
For the salvation of our heart
To search a spiritual connection so deep
Our faith may not need to depart

From an inner goodness your connection is found
In belief that's etched from within
As another dimension opens the inner mind
You will find the pardon from sin

Only with heartfelt compassion of man
Can God ever truly reside
For He has the eye that sees it all
From which you cannot hide

Continued overleaf...

If you are true to yourself and fellow brother
Then God may come to you
But if you thrive within the devil's web
Condemn you is what he will do

For if he opens the book of revelation
An event that has been foretold
The reckless ones with blackened hearts
To the devil will be sold

But for the good and pure or simple ones
Who pray for peace and love
The final act of prophecy for God
Will raise them high above

A Moral Judgement

The case before the court
Is the very first of its kind
As it tries the inner morals
And the minds of mankind

So before passing judgement
I need a psychological report
For I sense a terrible problem
Of mass human default

I will take a look
At the minds of the rich
For now I need to see
What really makes them tick

Through self-importance
Does ignorance persist?
Through dissected hearts
Can souls really exist?

With a division of unity
Through a gloating eye
Does the flag of luxury
Need to fly so high?

Continued overleaf...

Do you need to flaunt
All that you have got?
Do you need it all
While the peasants rot?

Now I have read the blank report
From a shallow empty mind
The only real verdict
Has been the easiest to find

In a narrow-minded view
Your real life will drown
Living in blind belief
You are the lord of the town

But in the end my friend
The tables always turn
For you have unearthed
A forced rise of the worm

Who only really wants
The ability to freely exist
But has now turned to crime
For he simply cannot resist

So the sentence then has already been passed
A shadow of crime is the one that you cast
Like frightened rats in a city zone
Where it is no longer safe to walk alone

A wealthy lust is an awful sin
Now we must pray for our next of kin
Widen your eyes and open your soul
Let the natural goodness take control

Live by those morals then you may see
With a fairer balance we could all be free

Play The Game

In visions through a child's eyes
It's no surprise
If you see what you want to see
Lost in reflections of a life once known
The child has grown
As it follows a destiny

Driving through a cloud of illusion
Caught in confusion
It shouldn't really be
Reach inside the inner mind
For there you will find
The one and only key

When the flame is burning out
Upon life's roundabout
It's a world of fantasy
Did Alice break the looking glass?
To play or pass
Through whose reality?

What do we know and what do we feel?
What is real?
Who can say?
What lies in a world redesigned?
What do you find
When living goes astray?

Who throws the dice in paradise?
Or casts a stone in the world unknown
Whose game do you play?
Who offers truth without the proof
Or sings the song with the words all wrong
In illusions of today?
Who pays the price in sacrifice?

Who's all alone when the mind is blown?
Who seeks a better way?
Who is the thief of true belief?
Who sells the soul, who's in control?
Who's seen a brighter day?

With open eyes it's no surprise
It's still your game to play
For if the way is known
Instead of shown
The light will lead the way
Break through the lies and realise
What life can truly be

For if the love is lost
Who counts the cost?
In peace and harmony
Seek the truth, find the proof
Open the inner eye
Look within, sink or swim
But know the reasons why.

Stormy Waters

I want to be alive
Within the rhythm of life
I want to be so free
Not living on the edge of a knife
With no more stormy waters
Or burdens on my back
With an eye looking forward
Where white never turns to black

I want to see a life
Where a light is shining
I want to find myself
In a magical silver lining
With no more troubles
And a living guarantee
With no more crazy wars
Only peace for eternity

I want to open my eyes
And see the rising sun
I want to truly feel
My race is nearly won
With no more hurting
Just wrapped in loving feeling
Without the inner pain
Or emotion ever sent reeling

I want to be so free
Where the water's always flowing
I want to finally know
Where am I really going?
With no more drifting on
Or the rolling of the dice
Without the weight of worry
Just living in paradise

Magic Carpet Ride

Who fits a magic carpet
Right beneath your feet?
Whose arms are wrapped around you
Where kisses taste so sweet

Love can last forever
If a true seed is sown
The love can be eternal
If the way is shown

If the heart is never torn apart
The feelings growing stronger
If the soul is tight
And the rhythm is right
Love will last for longer

When you see what you cannot see
Your eyes are open wide
If the light is bright
But doesn't blind the sight
Then it's a magic carpet ride.

Light Of Love

In a world of so much heartache
In a world of so much pain
Through love you find the answer
For there's nothing else to gain

Without love there is no reason
Without love you're all alone
Let it shine into your soul
'Cos a heart's not made of stone

Don't fight anger with anger
Try not to lose your head
Love is your greatest power
If it shines from you instead

If love grows cold in others
When eyes are pearls of ice
Never break the power of love
Just forgive in sacrifice

Stand tall against the evil
It's the way to break it down
None can ever withstand you
If the love in you is sound

Continued overleaf...

When someone tries to hurt you
The devil's got their soul
Forgiveness is the only power
If love is really in control
It keeps the fire burning
The light of love within
It is the power of life
For it governs everything

Love is the inner light
That shines within the dark
It feeds upon the power
And ignites the inner spark

The world keeps on turning
Round and round and round
When the love conquers all
Then your heaven will be found

The Power Of Christmas

The Christmas bells are ringing
Amid the joyous sounds of singing
A smiling face, an open heart,
As many worries will duly depart

The festive season of peace and love
A gifted light from Heaven above
People full of heartfelt greeting
Embraced together with families meeting

Christmas comes but once a year
To fill the souls with loving cheer
And light the life in which we live
Forgetting troubles with desire to give

Forgiveness is offered through open connection
The spirit of Jesus in full resurrection
Briefly unites us together as one
Remembering the birth of a special Son

Continued overleaf...

As the magic truly fills the air
Creating such harmony without a care
Feeling the light of a loving embrace
Is the gift He gave to the human race!

Enchanting power conjures the feeling
That sends the emotional senses reeling
As the light of Christ still shines so strong
Within its presence we see no wrong

If Christmas creates that one special day
Then Jesus Christ has never gone away
Upon a cross He was trussed and nailed
Through the light of Christmas He never failed

He spreads that light across the earth
Shining brightly in remembrance of His birth
Holding so many in mesmerised gladness
Reflecting a life without the sadness

The Magic Of Christmas

On Christmas morning, as the day is dawning
The spirit of Jesus enters the soul
A reaching light, that burns so bright
Bringing fruit into everyone's bowl
The time for sharing, a reason for caring
A light pulls the strings of the heart
Love shines through, with compassion that's true
In feelings the magic of Christmas will start
On Christmas day, the children will play
Whilst the elders find laughter and smile
Happiness is found, with a natural sound
Not having seen such joy for a while
With harmony at home, very few are alone
The unification of a great human family
Together as one, beneath a life-giving sun
All entwined in a peace-loving amenity
On Christmas night, the power of light
Still shines from a darkened sky
Throughout the day, it never goes away
So uplifting it could make many cry
The spirit of Jesus brings Christmas to please us
Touching the love within us all
On one special day, we could hope and pray
That from such magic we would never fall

A Loving Embrace

We could ask upon a special night
As to whether we truly believe
When most will feel a magical light
That ignites on Christmas Eve.

Goodwill to all men touches the soul
Whilst happiness fills the mind
The heart is opened as it loses control
Where emotions are redesigned.

As the spirit of Christmas engulfs the land
Good tidings are offered to all
In peaceful harmony, united we stand
The stout, the short, and the tall.

Peace on earth for a single day
With compassion for one another
Love is in the words we say
Whilst offering the hand of a brother.

Christmas becomes an enchanting gift
Bonding the hearts of a human race
The time for healing many a rift
Through feeling a loving embrace.

A Shining Star

Star of David shines through the night
Over a manger where the baby lay
Three wise men have followed its light
Bringing gifts, they kneel and pray

The baby Jesus was a special one
Enlightened in spiritual feeling
He brought a light and all was done
To fill the earth with believing

Miracles and healings within his power
Where the magic was truly seen
He could touch a dying wilted flower
And return it to a vibrant green

Wine from water and life from death
Through a spiritual transformation
Gifted hands with enchanted breath
Yet suffering such condemnation

Trying to prove what is hard to believe
Giving his life in order to save us
We remember his name on Christmas Eve
For the shining star is Jesus

Returning The Child

The childhood is a time of innocence
Where only pureness reigns in the mind
When it's gone is it gone forever
In the wicked life a child will find?

With the mind corrupted by all around it
Darkness begins to grow inside
Innocence gives way in a bid for survival
An existence that opens the eyes so wide

Clouded visions form the lure of temptation
Presented by a contorted society
The greed and desire manifests from within
As a life is filled with such needless anxiety

Dog eat dog see the unity vanish
No more protection from the arms of love
Harmony destroyed in a distorted passion
Losing sight of the peaceful white dove

Then come the addictions of a misled race
To numb away troubles we freely create
Constant pressure weighs a tortured soul
Until we are able and willing to desecrate

Do we seek the truth or just carry along
Within the evils delivered upon us?
Do we submit within the corrupted mind
Or find guidance from the words of Jesus?

A child we are born and a child must return
With goodness restored to the heart and soul
Winning the fight to become pure once again
If the wisdom ever truly seizes control

Placed on this earth with many truths to find
Was the purpose of the human existence
Not to surrender the soul to the devil of life
And continue living in blinded persistence

Enter the mind in search of the light
Abandon temptation in restrictive chains
Seek for the answers of a natural world
For that is the hope that always remains

Instructions are laid in the Holy Bible
A book that's forgotten and so easily defiled
But if you truly believe in God above
You must return to the Lord of the child

Continued overleaf...

Take a moral heart and a soul so pure
With righteousness in all that is done
So the innocence of childhood is finally restored
Flowing in goodness and unified under the sun

To ignore those rules the life will end
To uphold them brings a promise of more
Do we actually know where the truth really lies
Can we ever know there's no kingdom for sure?

The prophecy of disaster is already foretold
Horsemen cast plagues upon the age of men
Nation to rise against nation in the final hour
Visions hand-written by the enlightened pen

To believe is a choice all are free to make
Even though they may well be reviled
If the light shines brightly within the soul
Then the soul will return as a child.

A Prayer For The World

When we see such desecration
Upon our fragile earth
Do we blame the eternal mother
Or consider our own worth?

Through the course of evolution
The hands of man were spawned
With his curious twitching fingers
A special breed was formed

Man walks upon the grace of nature
She offered the gift of living
But as he paves his modern roads
Will she ever be forgiving?

Is man so blind he cannot see?
Whilst destroying nature's reality
By neglecting his ruling power
To boldly stand upon the helm

Can the created ever be the creator?
Without an unnatural overload
To change and alter the living earth
Is following a treacherous road

Continued overleaf...

Will the mind now see the wrong
Whilst desire is dissolving the head
As the power of nature is closing in
Because of bullshit man's been fed

If the environment finally collapses
Where do we lie the blame?
If the truth is found within the soul
Then where do we hide the shame?

It is time to remove the blindness
Then rub the weary eyes
To see the natural living picture
Before it fades and dies

If we say a prayer for the world
With feeling from the heart
Follow it up with moral action
Then that would be a start

Mother nature makes the rules
Not the meddling hands of man
If he cannot abide by the laws of life
Then he alone will carry the can

A sacred world of mystical wonder
Is cast by a magic spell
Scientifically changed and altered
It now sounds its warning bell

Signs are there so loud and clear
Nature is crying in despair
So it brings upon us the retribution
For the pollution of our air

The gloves are off, the fight has begun
So if the heart does really care
Make the move to right the wrong
Whilst saying that little prayer

A Season's End

When the winter snows are gently falling
Floating flakes upon a leaden sky
A pure white carpet covers the ground
Ice on the air stings the eye

Vegetation is dead and frozen over
A hibernation for a living earth
One cycle of life has reached its end
In preparation for a wondrous rebirth

First rays of spring engulf the land
And awakening in vibrant colour
Plants reach out to feel the light
The magic of our gracious mother

She comes alive in floral bloom
A brighter sun begins to smile
The gift of nature returns once more
Flooding the earth in nature's style

The summer brings the beaming faces
Lifted in heart-warming sunshine
The growing cycle will be completed
For nature knows the natural time

Skies are clearing and seas are blue
Where a radiance fills the air
A shimmering light is all around
Presenting the earth with its flair

Autumn trees changing to golden brown
Life draining from their leaves
Branches dressed with twig-like fingers
Outlines on a gentle breeze

Harvest time is nature's gift
The season for a feast
A sun is waning from the sky
But will return from the East

One year on a revolution is complete
The magical cycle of nature
A season screen of changing images
So why did we ever deface her?

Desolation is a season we don't yet know
But if it comes will always remain
No longer seeing a kaleidoscope of colour
The scene would stay the same

The season's end would end all seasons
If an environment fades away
Preserve the magic of a precious earth
Reach into your heart today

A Magical Eye

If we could see through a magical eye
That looks down upon the earth
Then it may be easy to comprehend
The true fashioning of our birth

Were we made or did we evolve
Who is our true creator?
For whatever belief we choose to hold
None can deny the power of nature

Is she natural or of a higher making
The magic is wrapped in enigma
Forces of wonder in a mysterious realm
Answers we cannot deliver

Man is nature as nature is man
Entwined in the same fascination
His gift was life upon the earth
The master of all creation

By whose authority should he thrive?
Controlling the world around him
Who should he obey on a course of life
When the ozone is wearing thin?

A time for answers is upon us all
By discarding the unsaid rules
The balance of nature has been upset
Racing around like mindless fools

The natural magic of a living world
Is trampled in reckless motion
Power of God or a spiritual touch
Has lost the true devotion

Man has risen to rule the roost
His Creator is severely neglected
He makes his laws as he recreates
Tampering with what was perfected

Mankind has learned the lessons from life
But one has escaped the mind
By altering the power supporting us all
Only retribution we will find

Does man believe he can change the force?
That created the magical earth
Does he think he can rule the power
Responsible for his own birth?

Hope

Hope will lay within all of our hearts
As either passion or desire
One will yearn the goodness in life
The other fuelling the devil's fire

Hope that's applied to the living world
Is the real hope we need
When it's cast for personal gain
It will drive a selfish greed

Hope for salvation for sacred earth
Is a natural human instinct
If a desiring mind then abandons it
Mankind may become extinct

Hope that's formed through wrongful action
Becomes a kind of little prayer
That if something could change the vision
A life would then be fair

Hope that is cast through desperation
Is wishing from the mind
That the madness all around the world
Had never been designed

Hope that's born for self-satisfaction
Is actually our desire
A darker side of the living soul
That easily creates a liar

Hope for a unified human race
Is the greatest of them all
For in compassionate love and harmony
The need for hope would fall

Inner Breath

Breathe in, breathe in deep
What is it that you feel?
Breathe in, close your eyes
Are the inner senses real?

Breathe in, lay down on your back
Resting your body down
Breathe in, so as to let it in
The life that's all around

Just relax, then release the mind
Feel the pressures melt away
Just relax, through a nasal inhale
Eyelids blocking the light of day

Just relax, draw a deep breath
Hold it in for the longest time
Just relax, then gently let it out
Feel the body float and realign

Floating, within the mind
Draw only a little air
Floating, whilst holding it in
Until you feel no living care

Floating, surrender your soul
From all conscious thought alleviate
Floating, drift under the spell
Soon you will begin to meditate

Breathe in, for that is the key
Feel the power of the sky
Breathe in, inhale the life force
You may need to try and try

Breathe in, feel the spirit rise
The mind will be enlightened
Breathe in, trust your inner self
Never once become the frightened

Feel the power rise from within
Let the spirit take control
Feel the power within yourself
Remove the barriers of your soul

Feel the power in the air
The lifeline of mother nature
Feel the power of natural life
There's no need to recreate her.